Contents

W0359786

Chapter One

Rosso

Rosso the gypsy boy lived in a caravan. It was not one of those beautiful old gypsy caravans that you see in pictures or photos of the English countryside in summer. No, Rosso's caravan was a long, modern box and stood not in a field but in a scrapyard at the end of a little street in Battersea, South London. He lived in the caravan with his grandfather, Jake, and their family name was Smith, like many gypsies.

Rosso was fifteen years old and had been living with his grandfather for almost seven years. His mother worked in a circus, so for most of the year she travelled around Britain – and sometimes abroad – with her job. She wanted Rosso to have a better chance in life, which meant that he could not travel with her. So he lived with his grandfather and went to Battersea Comprehensive School, like all the other boys and girls in the area.

But Rosso was not like the other boys and girls. He was a gypsy, and everybody knows what gypsies are like: black hair, brown eyes, dark skin. Gypsies are lazy people who do as little work as possible and who live in caravans, not houses like other people. It did not matter that many of the boys and girls at Rosso's school were black, or brown and that their grandparents had come to London from Barbados, Trinidad, Jamaica, from Africa, India or Pakistan. They lived in proper houses with proper parents, and they had brothers and sisters – sometimes a lot of brothers and sisters. They were not lazy gypsies who lived in scrapyards between the railway lines.

The other children did not often play with Rosso, so he was often very lonely. If his grandfather was not at home when he got back from school, Rosso made himself something to eat and sat on the steps of their caravan, watching the trains. They were just ordinary commuter trains – nothing romantic – but Rosso often thought about his mother and wished that he could take one of these trains and join her. He had a father, but he had not seen him for over six years, and there were reasons why he tried not to think too much about his father.

Rosso's grandfather was not a rich man. When people asked him what his job was, he always said "used-car dealer" but most of the old cars in the scrapyard at the end of Culvert Place, Battersea, would never be "used" again. The people who came to Jake Smith's yard were only looking for parts for their own old, used cars: a starter motor, perhaps, or a wing mirror for a Mini, or something more exotic, like leather seats for an old Jaguar, or a speedometer for a Triumph Spitfire. If Jake could not find the parts which the people wanted, he drove off in the old Ford van and visited other scrapyards all over South London until he found the parts they needed. It took a lot of time, and the people rarely came back.

"There are too many scrapyards in London anyway," he said to Rosso sadly. "When you grow up, Rosso, you must find a better job."

"Such as what?"

"I don't know – but any regular work is better than this! You get regular wages, paid holidays and a pension at the end of it! What do I get? Lumbago at sixty-five, and I'm still working a 70-hour week!" But secretly he loved his cars, and so did Rosso.

Rosso loved playing with the old cars in the yard. When Jake bought an old car that could still run he sometimes let Rosso drive it slowly round and round the yard. "I learnt to drive when I was twelve!" he said, and he had taught his grandson at about the same age.

There was one very special car in the yard. Rosso's father's car. It had been Jake's car, too, and was almost as old as Rosso's father. It was a red and cream Riley RMB. Jake kept it in a small garage at the end of the yard, but once a month, usually on a

Sunday, he drove it out into the sunshine (if there was any sunshine) and allowed Rosso to wash the windows or polish the chrome.

"When your father comes home," Jake often said to Rosso, "the Riley must be ready for him. It was my car and one day it will be yours." It was the only time Jake ever talked about his son Raymond, Rosso's father.

One day in March something strange happened to Rosso. After school he went to Woolworth's in Battersea Park Road and bought a big red notebook. He had never kept a diary before, but today he sat on the steps of the caravan in the afternoon sunshine with his grandfather's old alsatian dog Jason and began to write:

March 9th

There is a new girl in our class. She is fifteen, like me, and her name is Julia. She is from Angermunde (I think that's how she spells it) in Germany and has long blond hair and blue eyes. She sat next to me in class because there was nowhere else for her to sit. None of the other kids wants to sit next to me.

Her father is an engineer and he is working in London for two years. They live in one of the new flats in Francis Chichester Way. We had lunch together in the cafeteria and talked a lot. Her English is not too good and she says she has trouble with our London accent (Ha Ha!), so I promised to help her with her homework.

I walked home with her. She asked me about my family and I lied. I said my mother and father both worked away from home, and that I lived with my grandmother and grandfather in a small house in Culvert Place (at least I didn't lie about the street name!) She said she would like to come and visit me tomorrow.

What shall I do if she really comes? I am a gypsy and I live in a caravan in a scrapyard!

Chapter two

Julia

When Julia got home after school that afternoon, she told her mother about the nice boy she had met at school. Mrs Witzkow was pleased that her daughter had found a friend on her first day at her new school. Life had not been easy for the Witzkows. Her husband Jürgen had lost his job at the small factory in Angermünde soon after the reunification of Germany.

The family had moved to a new job in Düsseldorf, but the new job was not what Mr Witzkow wanted, so they soon had to move again – to Hechingen in South Germany this time. Julia was their only child, and Mr and Mrs Witzkow wanted the best for their daughter. But they did not have much money, and sometimes 'the best' was quite expensive.

Julia loved riding. In Brandenburg there had been plenty of horses to ride, but in Hechingen, their new home, riding was an expensive hobby. Everything was more expensive in the West: their flat, their new car, the new colour TV and stereo video recorder, new clothes ...

Then one evening Mr Witzkow had come home with more bad news.

"Wir müssen wieder umziehen. Die Firma will, dass ich für zwei Jahre nach London gehe."

"London! Aber wir sind doch erst hierher gezogen!" cried Julia, *"und ich habe gerade neue Freunde gefunden! Außerdem kann ich kaum Englisch sprechen!"*

"Tut mir Leid," said Mr Witzkow, *"aber wenn ich nicht nach London gehe, verliere ich meinen Job!"*

Mrs Witzkow was unhappy, too, but she had not been able to find a job in Hechingen – she was a kindergarten teacher – and she knew they would have to go to London. She would be able to practise her school English at last!

The firm helped the Witzkows to find somewhere to live near their factory in Battersea. It was not the nicest place to live, but it was a modern flat on the second floor of a new building. Julia preferred living in a flat. The small houses in Battersea looked old and dirty, and there were so many black people and Asians! Even Rosso, the boy she had sat next to that first day at school, had dark skin – but such beautiful dark eyes! And long, black hair. And he talked about such interesting things …

Her mother listened while she talked about her new friend. This boy with the strange name sounded more like an Italian than an English boy.

"Lade doch Rosso mal zu uns ein," she said. If Julia was so interested in this boy, perhaps she and Jürgen should meet him.

"Er hat mir versprochen, mir bei den Hausaufgaben zu helfen."

"Nett von ihm! Wo wohnt er denn?"

"In einem kleinen Haus in Culvert Place. Das muss in der Nähe von der Culvert Road sein, wo unsere Schule ist."

"Hmm."

The next morning Julia went to school early, but she did not go straight there. She walked down Austin Road and Rowditch Lane to Culvert Street. But where was Culvert Place? She could see her school at one end of Culvert Street on the right, but on the left was only a low, black tunnel under the busy railway lines. Above the tunnel was a sign: TO 1-13 CULVERT STREET & CULVERT PLACE.

Suddenly Julia heard somebody coming along the tunnel. She quickly walked back to the corner of Rowditch Lane. Then she turned around and walked back just as Rosso came out of the tunnel into the sunshine. He did not see her, but she called out: "Rosso! Wait for me!"

Rosso turned quickly round, but he did not seem happy to see Julia. He looked quite angry, in fact. "What are you doing here?"

"The same as you. I'm going to school."

Rosso stopped and looked at her with his dark eyes. Did he think she had been spying on him?

"Come on then. Hurry up, or we'll be late!"

Julia sat next to Rosso again, but he did not take much notice of her during English and maths. Then came break, and although they went into the playground together, Rosso did not say much to her, and after five minutes he just walked away and began to talk to somebody else.

History and French were the two lessons after break. Julia did not go to French lessons because she had to learn English quickly. She had a private English lesson with Mrs Pyne in a small room in another part of the school, and when the lesson was over Rosso had already left their classroom. He was not in the cafeteria for lunch, either, and Julia began to wonder what was wrong. The boy who had been so nice to her the day before was avoiding her! Why? She could not understand it.

The first lesson after lunch was PE, so she could not talk to Rosso much, but after PE they had handicrafts. This was one of the pupils' favourite subjects. They could do woodwork or metalwork, and they were doing a project on models. Each boy and girl had to make a model in wood or metal: a wooden house or plane, a metal bridge or train. Rosso was making a model car.

Julia, who was new and had nothing to do yet, walked over and looked at Rosso while he worked on his model.

"It's beautiful."

"Hmm." Rosso did not look up from his work.

"Is it a special car? It looks very old."

"It's my father's car."

"Does he drive it every day?"

"No, it's in the garage at home. My father doesn't work in London. I told you that yesterday."

"Sorry. I forgot." She watched him for a few minutes. He

was painting the roof black. He said nothing, so Julia asked: "Can I see the car when I come round this afternoon?"

Rosso stopped painting and looked up at her. His dark eyes suddenly opened very wide. "This afternoon?"

"You said I could visit you at your house this afternoon."

"Not this afternoon. It isn't convenient."

Julia did not know the word 'convenient', but she understood it. He did not want her to come. "But we can walk home together after school?"

"If you like," was all he said. Then he looked down at his model again. The teacher, Mr Williams, came over to give the new girl something to do, so they had no time to talk until school was over.

Rosso was very quiet as they walked back to Julia's flat. The sky was dark and it was beginning to rain.

When they reached the corner of Francis Chichester Way, Rosso said: "I think I should go home now. It's raining."

"Don't you want to come in and meet my mother?"

Rosso thought for a second, then said: "Not today, Julia. Maybe tomorrow. Bye!" And he walked off back down the road. Julia walked on sadly. Something was wrong. Was it her? She had no idea. She just felt very unhappy.

"War's schön in der Schule heute?" her mother asked.

"Nein!" said Julia, and went quickly into her room.

CHAPTER THREE

Tell me no lies

The next day was Saturday, and Mrs Witzkow sent Julia to do the shopping. She was busy and her husband was at work – even on a Saturday morning.

When she had done the shopping, Julia began to walk back home, but when she reached the corner of Culvert Road and Rowditch Lane she did not turn left but walked straight on into the dark tunnel that led under the railway lines to the south end of Culvert Road and Culvert Place. At the end of the tunnel she stopped and looked around. In front of her was a road which went under another railway bridge.

There were no houses in this part of Culvert Street, but there was another short street on her left with the usual small, dirty-brown terraced houses in it. So this was Culvert Place! At the end of the street, through the open gates, Julia could see a scrapyard full of old cars, metal parts and other rubbish. There was a big modern caravan at the back of the yard – the most modern thing in the street. Beside the caravan an old man was looking for something in a large box full of metal parts. An old alsatian dog was sitting in the early March sunshine. On the steps of the caravan sat a dark-haired boy. He was writing something in a big red notebook.

It was Jason the dog who saw Julia first. He got up slowly – he was an old dog – and began to walk towards the gate. Rosso looked up when he heard Jason move and saw a blond girl with two heavy shopping bags at the corner of the street. They stared at each other for almost a minute before one of them moved. Then they both moved at once. Julia turned away, picked up her bags and disappeared into the tunnel. Rosso closed his book and ran after her. He caught up with her at the far end of the tunnel. Without a word he took one of the heavy shopping bags out of Julia's hand, and they both walked on in silence.

"Well," said Rosso after a while, "now you know."

"Know?"

"Now you know all about me."

"I know nothing about you, Rosso."

"You know that I lied to you about living in a house. We're Romanies – gypsies! The kids at school would have told you about us sooner or later, I suppose. Gypsies don't live in houses like other people. We live in caravans. My grandad runs a scrapyard."

"Why are you so angry, Rosso? It's not my fault, it's not your fault ... "

"It's nobody's fault. But it's the reason why the other kids at school don't like me much. Why did you come round this morning? Why are you spying on me? Why can't you just leave me alone?"

"I'm not spying on you, Rosso. After what happened yesterday I thought you didn't like me any more. I like you, Rosso, and I want to be your friend."

"Why did you run away, then?"

"Run away?"

"Yes, why did you run away when you saw me in the yard? Why didn't you come in and say hello – and meet my grandfather and the dog – and have a look at our caravan? It has got a proper toilet and bathroom. You mustn't think that we don't wash occasionally. Why did you run away?"

Julia thought for a second. "I don't know. Perhaps I was frightened. I wasn't expecting to see you."

Rosso said nothing. They had reached the corner of Francis Chichester Way. They stopped and put down the shopping bags. Julia looked down at the street sign.

"Who was Francis Chichester?" she asked.

"He was a yachtsman. He sailed around the world – alone – about twenty-five years ago."

"Alone?"

"Yes. All round the world – quite alone – in a small yacht,"

Julia said nothing. But she was thinking about herself and Rosso. They were both alone, but in different ways.

"Let's start again – let's be good friends!" said Rosso. "We can have secrets if you like, but no more lies."

"OK, " said Julia. "'Ask me no questions and I'll tell you no lies'!"

"Where did you learn that?" asked Rosso in surprise. Julia's English was improving very quickly.

"In my private English lesson – Mrs Pyne! See you later, Rosso." Julia picked up both shopping bags and turned away.

"Wait a minute, Julia!" Rosso shouted after her. "Can't I come and meet your parents?"

"My father is at work this morning, and my mother is very busy." Then she remembered Rosso's phrase. "And anyway, 'it's not convenient' today. Come tomorrow afternoon after lunch and help me with my English!"

And before he could say 'no', she had disappeared into the entrance of Number Ten.

Chapter Four

Shorty

On Sunday afternoon Rosso helped Julia with her English homework. When they finished it was only three o'clock. The Witzkows had asked Rosso to stay for tea, but tea was not ready yet, so Julia and Rosso went out for a walk in Battersea Park. They talked about the differences between Germany and Britain. Julia did not like London very much.

"It's so big!"

"London is all right. If you know your own part of London, you can live there and forget the rest – except the West End, of course."

"The West End?"

"Yes. Oxford Street, Piccadilly, the shops, cinemas and theatres. Haven't you been to the West End yet?"

"We went on a sightseeing tour when we first arrived, but we just saw the old buildings like the Tower and Buckingham Palace. Will you show me the West End?"

"Yes, of course! What about tomorrow – after school?"

"Fine!" and that was that.

When Rosso got home after tea with the Witzkows, Jake was sitting on the sofa reading a car magazine. Rosso sat down at the table with his red notebook and began to write. His grandfather looked up. "Homework?"

"No. Something private."

"Hmm," Jake turned back to his magazine and there was silence for a few minutes before he spoke again. "Shorty Mulligan was here again while you were out."

"Shorty? What did he want?"

"What he always wants. He wanted to know if you would join his gang."

"The answer is still 'no'."

"That's what I told him. Stay away from Shorty and his gang, Rosso. They're no good."

"I know that, Grandad." He went on writing in his diary. "The police caught Shorty's brother Patrick last week – shoplifting in Woolworth's."

"That's probably why they're so interested in you. Patrick will be 'out of action' for quite a time!"

Rosso said nothing. He was busy writing. Jake watched him over the top of his magazine for a few minutes. Over the last few days Rosso had changed. He was quieter, more serious. He was growing up fast. Jake thought about his own youth and smiled to himself. Then he got up and switched the TV on just in time for the seven o'clock news.

After school the next day Rosso and Julia took the number 19 bus to Oxford Circus and walked along Oxford Street. Julia had never seen so many big shops and stores – not even in Berlin or Düsseldorf. There were no private cars in Oxford Street, only buses and taxis.

At Marble Arch they turned left down Park Lane and walked past the famous hotels with Hyde Park on their right. At Hyde Park Corner they turned left again into Piccadilly and walked back towards Piccadilly Circus, where they stopped to look at the young people sitting and talking on the steps of the Eros statue.

"Londoners say that if you just stand here and wait, you'll meet everybody you ever knew in your life," said Rosso.

"Do you really believe that?"

"It's possible – if you wait long enough!"

They both laughed.

"Let's not wait, Rosso," said Julia. "There are some people I wouldn't like to meet again."

"Me, too," said Rosso. It was just at that moment that he saw Shorty Mulligan and two of the boys from his gang. Shorty had already seen Rosso. He was a year older than Rosso and Julia, but almost a head shorter. He had short, sandy hair and small green eyes in a round face. It was easy to see why his nickname was 'Shorty'.

"Hi, Rosso! Who's the girlfriend?"

"This is Julia. She's in my class at school. She's from Germany and she's *not* my girlfriend."

Shorty smiled. It was not a nice smile. "I was at your place yesterday but you were out. I came to ask you about joining the gang."

"The answer is still 'no', Shorty."

"That's a pity. We could use you in the gang, Rosso. Like your dad's cousin Gerry used your dad ..."

For a second Julia thought that Rosso was going to hit Shorty. But Shorty's two friends came closer, and Rosso changed his mind. "You shut up about my father! There are plenty of things I could say about *your* father – and they would all be true! Come on, Julia. Let's go home!" And before she could say anything, Rosso had taken her by the hand and was pulling her down the steps to the Underground station. He bought two tickets and did not speak until they were waiting on the platform for the train.

"Shorty Mulligan and his gang are the next generation of small-time crooks: shoplifters, car thieves, filling-station hold-ups ... They want me to join their gang because I can drive a car. My grandad taught me to drive in our yard."

Julia was fascinated. "You mean they really do things like that?"

"Shorty's brother Patrick was caught shoplifting last week, and Shorty will be next. Did you see that Swatch he was wearing? I expect it was stolen, too. His uncle has been to prison once or twice."

"Prison?" Julia sounded shocked. "And what did he mean about your father, Rosso?"

But Rosso only said: "Here comes our train."

Julia said nothing. She remembered his promise – and the useful phrase which Mrs Pyne had taught her: 'Ask me no questions and I'll tell you no lies'.

On Tuesday after school, Rosso took Julia home to meet his grandfather and to make friends with Jason the alsatian. Julia was surprised to see that the caravan was as comfortable as a small flat. There were two small bedrooms, a larger living-room, a kitchen and a proper bathroom.

Everything was clean and tidy: "A place for everything and everything in its place," said Jake with a smile while he was making the tea. "We gypsies wouldn't be able to live in caravans if we were untidy people."

While they were having tea, Jake told Julia something about the life of the Romany gypsies.

"They say that gypsies come from Northern India," he began, "but I was born in a caravan somewhere on the road – in Oxfordshire, I think – and my parents came from the country around Leicester. When I was Rosso's age we were still 'travellers'. We moved around the country, and I only went to school in the winter for a few months every year until I was fourteen, but I can read and write as well as most people. Some people don't like us, although we don't do them any harm. My grandfather bought and sold horses but my father bought and sold cars. That was before the war. I learnt how to repair cars while I was in the army. That's how I started this scrapyard." He pointed to a few photos on the wall. "That's the yard when I started up twenty years ago. And that one is me and Rosso's father when he was Rosso's age."

Another of the photos showed a car like the model which Rosso was making at school. A young man (Rosso's father?) and a young woman in their wedding clothes were standing in front of it. The woman was carrying a large bunch of flowers. "What a lovely wedding photo!" cried Julia.

"Yes. Rosso's mum and dad. We still use the old Riley for weddings. Some couples like to hire an old car like that on their wedding day. Very classy!"

Rosso went into his bedroom and came back a few moments later with a small box of photos. "My mum works in a circus," he began. "Would you like to see some photos of her?"

So Julia spent the next half hour looking at photos of Rosso's mother, 'The Wonderful Ilona', standing on the back of a galloping horse or high in the air on a trapeze, or just smiling at the camera. She was beautiful. She had the same black hair and dark eyes as Rosso.

"Do you see her often?" Julia asked.

"During the summer holidays. I go to stay with her – if she's in Britain. The circus is closed in the summer anyway. We have a wonderful time, but it's always too short."

"And while he's away, I have to look after myself!" said Jake. But the way he said it made Rosso and Julia laugh.

Not long after that Julia looked at her watch and said it was time for her to go home.

Rosso walked back with her. He was quiet. When they reached the Witzkows' flat he said: "I expect I should tell you something about my father ..."

"Not now, Rosso. It's your secret. Tell me about your father when you want to talk about him."

CHAPTER FIVE

London spring

March turned into April. The days were longer now, and Julia and Rosso spent more time outside in the warm spring sunshine (Julia was surprised that it didn't rain all the time in London!). They often went to Battersea Park or walked along the River Thames.

London is a city of parks and open spaces, and Rosso and Julia explored them one by one: Hyde Park with its big old trees, where they loved to take Jason for walks. Green Park between Piccadilly and Buckingham Palace, where they often sat and watched the people walking home from work. St James's Park, where they fed bread to the ducks and flamingos. Kensington Gardens with its statue of Peter Pan. Even Hampstead Heath, several miles to the north of Battersea and really like a piece of open countryside where they could almost forget London, although it lay all around them, unseen. The evenings became longer and to them it seemed that the sun was rarely covered by rain clouds that spring.

Rosso was no longer lonely. Jake noticed the difference, too, and most of the other boys and girls at school smiled when they saw the two 'outsiders', the gypsy boy and the German girl, walking out of the school gate together. Only one of the boys at school seemed jealous of the friendship: Shorty Mulligan.

He and some of the boys in the gang teased Rosso about his friendship with Julia. Rosso pretended that he did not mind, but he kept thinking: "Thank goodness the Easter holidays start soon. Maybe then we'll get some peace from Shorty and his gang!"

After school on the last evening before the holidays Rosso, who had been saving up his money, took Julia to a hamburger restaurant in Chelsea, and afterwards they walked along the river to one of his favourite places – a quiet little park on the north bank of the Thames. They sat and watched the boats moving up and down the river. There were some houseboats along the bank. It must be very romantic to live here, thought Julia. The people who own these houseboats must be very rich! Then she realized how similar a houseboat must be to Rosso's caravan.

"They call this part of Chelsea 'World's End'," said Rosso. "I don't know why, but I expect it was a very lonely place hundreds of years ago."

They sat in silence for a few minutes, watching the water. It was beginning to get dark, and Julia thought it was time to go home.

"I've got a present for you," said Rosso, feeling a little awkward, and took a small piece of beautifully carved wood out of his pocket.

Julia looked at it. "It's beautiful! What is it?"

"A whistle – No! Don't blow it now! It's a special Romany whistle. You must only blow it if you need help. If there are any Romanies near, they will come and help you. It's very old. My mother gave it to me ..."

"Oh, Rosso! Are you sure ...?"

"Yes. Keep it. Then if anything happens ..."

Then they walked slowly back a different way – over Battersea Bridge. Julia knew it was a longer route, but she said nothing. Rosso held her hand for most of the way.

CHAPTER SIX

Escape

The next day was the first day of the Easter holidays – a Saturday – and Rosso was polishing his father's Riley in the yard. Suddenly Jason began to growl. Rosso looked up and saw a stranger, a man of about fifty, at the gate. The man took a few steps towards Rosso but stopped when he saw the dog. Jason growled again, and the man took two steps back.

"Don't worry, Mister," said Rosso, who thought the man was a Saturday afternoon customer. "He doesn't bite. He's almost as old as me!"

The man came closer, although he still looked a bit worried. Then he walked up to the Riley and put his hand on the car's freshly polished chrome. "What a lovely old car! Is it for sale?"

"No," said Rosso. "This is my father's car. It's not for sale. You can hire it for weddings and things like that – with my grandfather as driver."

The man kept on looking at the car as if he had not heard, so Rosso tried again. "Can I help you at all?"

The man looked up and smiled. "I'd like to speak to your father. Is he at home?"

"You can speak to my grandfather. He owns the yard," said Rosso, pointing to the caravan. "He's in there."

The man went over to the caravan, knocked on the door and walked in. Rosso went on polishing the Riley.

Five minutes later the man left. He looked angry and said nothing to Rosso. Then Jake came out of the caravan looking angry, too.

"I've got to go and see somebody," he said. "When you put the Riley away, make sure you lock the garage. Don't leave the keys in the car, either!"

Rosso, who *always* locked the garage and *never* left the keys in the car, wanted to say something – or to ask Jake about the man – but Jake was already in the van. He usually told Rosso where he was going and when he would be back, but today he had said nothing. It was all very strange.

When he had finished polishing the car, Rosso backed it carefully into the garage, locked it and – just to be on the safe side – removed the rotor arm. Nobody could move the car now, not even with the key. The car was safe enough now, he thought. Then he went back into the caravan. There was nothing interesting on TV, and Julia was away with her parents for the weekend. She would be back on Sunday afternoon, and Rosso planned to show her more of London.

It was a fine day, so he thought he would take Jason for a walk in the park. But when he whistled for the dog there was no sign of him. Jake had probably taken him in the van. So Rosso went for a walk on his own. He stopped at a newspaper shop to buy his grandfather an evening paper and was halfway out of the shop before he saw the headlines. When he saw them he stopped dead, right in the middle of the doorway. An old woman who was just coming into the shop bumped into him.

"Can't you look where you're going?" she shouted angrily, but Rosso was not listening. He was reading the article below the headlines:

BULLION ROBBER ESCAPES

Gerry Smith, who was serving a fifteen-year sentence for armed robbery, escaped from Wandsworth Prison, London, yesterday. It is thought that Smith escaped in an ambulance from the prison hospital after changing places with another prisoner.

Seven years ago Smith and two accomplices robbed a bullion van taking gold and platinum bars from a bank in London to Heathrow Airport. Two of the men were caught soon afterwards with half the bullion, but the other half, worth at least £500,000, is still missing.

Gerry Smith, the leader of the gang, was sent to prison for fifteen years. His accomplices Sidney Mulligan and Albert Johnson came out of prison last year, and the police believe that they helped to organize Smith's escape. If this is true, the three men may already be on their way to the hidden gold.

A fourth man, Gerry Smith's cousin Raymond, was also suspected of being an accomplice. He was with Gerry Smith when he was caught, but Raymond Smith escaped after an exciting chase on the M1 motorway. Police suspect that he left the country soon after the robbery and has been living abroad ever since.

Police are concentrating their search for the escaped prisoner on the Leicester area.

Rosso knew why. Leicester was the town where most of his father's family lived. Raymond, Rosso's father, was living in France. Rosso knew that his father had had no part in the bullion robbery, but the police were still looking for him. Rosso had not seen him for seven years, although he knew that he still sent his mother money, and that his mother and father met secretly whenever Ilona's circus was in France or Belgium.

What would Jake say when he saw the paper? Would anyone at school remember the robbery, and that Gerry Smith was his father's cousin? Only Shorty Mulligan, probably, and he would not want to talk about the robbery because his uncle had gone to prison for his part in it. That was his secret. But what would Julia and her family think if they found out? This was what worried Rosso most of all.

Perhaps Julia would not see the article at all. She and her parents were away for the weekend, but they might see something about the escape on the TV news. He had promised not to lie to her again, but now his big secret was no longer a secret. If anyone told her about the bullion robbery she would know that his father had been involved in a serious crime ...

Rosso was just turning the corner into Culvert Place when he saw Shorty Mulligan – the last person he wanted to see – at the yard gate. Shorty was reading an article in a newspaper which seemed to be very interesting. When he saw Rosso he looked up and smiled.

"Hello, Rosso. I've just been reading about your father and his friends. Fine family ..." Shorty said no more. Rosso threw himself at him and the two boys began to fight. Suddenly each boy felt a strong hand on his shoulder as Jake, who had just arrived back in the van, pulled them apart.

"That's enough of that!" he said. "Rosso, come with me!"

"He started it!" shouted Shorty, feeling his nose.

"I expect he did. But you probably deserved it, and unless you want Rosso to finish it, just go home!"

Shorty walked away and Rosso followed Jake back into the

caravan. Jake looked at the newspaper in Rosso's hand.

"So you've read all about Gerry's escape, then?"

Rosso nodded and sat down. Jake knew already. Was that why the man had come to the yard this afternoon? The man had seemed familiar. Had it been Sidney Mulligan, Shorty's uncle? Jake said nothing for a moment. Then he took a deep breath and told Rosso the whole story.

Chapter seven

Not guilty

"Your father had nothing to do with the robbery, Rosso. I've always told you that, and it's true. Your father wasn't a crook. Your mother would never have allowed him to do anything criminal. The robbery was Gerry's idea."

"So what happened? How did Dad get involved? Why did you never tell me what really happened?"

"It was like this, Rosso. After the robbery the gang split up. Mulligan and Johnson took their half of the bullion, but were caught by the police a few days later. Gerry had the other half of the loot somewhere here in London. Johnson and Mulligan grassed on Gerry – that's why they only got eight years. They got out last year after only six – two years 'remission for good conduct'. Gerry got fifteen years because he didn't tell the police where the rest of the loot was. Mulligan and Johnson – or their friends – probably organized the escape to get a share of the loot. No one wants to wait fifteen years ..."

"But if they grassed on him, he'll be after their blood, won't he? He won't want to share his half of the loot with anyone, will he?"

"Look at it this way, Rosso. Gerry got fifteen years. No chance of remission for good conduct until he told the police where the rest of the bullion was. No, Rosso. Fifteen years – out in seven. Even if Gerry had escaped earlier there would have been no chance of getting to the rest of the bullion until the police got tired of watching every step he took. That could take years. He would need help – and who would be better than his old accomplices? Even if he could recover the loot on his own: what would he do with half a million quid in gold and platinum bars? It would weigh nearly half a ton! He wouldn't be able to carry it down to the bank, would he? He'd need friends – and quick. Don't forget that the other two have been out for over six months already. Plenty of time to arrange to sell the bullion if only they could get their hands on it!"

"So all Gerry has to do is take them to it? But surely the police know that, too. They're not stupid."

Jake said nothing, so Rosso changed the subject. "Who was that man who came here this afternoon?"

"Just somebody who was interested in the Riley. Why do you ask?"

"I thought I recognized him, that's all."

Jake said nothing. Rosso felt that his grandfather was not telling him everything he knew, but he said nothing. How strange that somebody should be interested in buying his father's car the day after the last bullion robber had escaped from prison! And was there a connection between the robbery and the Riley?

Wandsworth Prison was only a mile away from Battersea. Gerry Smith's accomplices had been from Clapham (one of them, Rosso knew, had been Shorty's Uncle Sidney). The bullion robbery was beginning to look like a very local affair. Perhaps the rest of the bullion was still hidden in the area, too. But where?

Rosso spoke again: "Was there any connection between the Riley and the police chase down the motorway?"

Jake said nothing for a while, and again Rosso thought that he was hiding something. Finally he spoke. "Yes, Rosso. You probably don't remember what happened – you were only about seven years old at the time and were still living with your parents near Leicester. On the evening after the robbery, Gerry rang your father from London and told him that he needed help. He didn't say what kind of help, but family is family, as we say. Perhaps he wanted to leave the country. Anyway, they agreed to meet at Newport Pagnell, that's a motorway service area halfway between London and Leicester. Your mother needed the car that evening, so your dad drove down in the old

Riley. They met at the service area and drove off in Gerry's car – a big Aston Martin. The police must have known the registration number of Gerry's car because they spotted it and began to follow it. They would never have caught them if Gerry's car hadn't run out of petrol. Your dad was so angry with Gerry that he drove the car into the side of a bridge so he could get out of the car but Gerry couldn't. Your dad has been hiding from the police ever since – somewhere in France."

There was silence for a minute, then Jake went on. "Although your dad used the Riley that night, it was still my car. A few days later I got a phone call from the motorway police to tell me that my car had been standing in the car park at the service area for almost a week. They were worried about vandals. Could I please come and move it? They didn't associate the car with your dad. After all, there must be millions of Smiths in Britain!"

"So you drove the car back here?"

"That's right, and it's been here ever since."

"But suppose the rest of the bullion is hidden in the car somewhere!"

Jake just laughed. "There's not enough room to hide much in those old cars. And anyway, I'd have noticed it – or you would have. The car was nowhere near London when the robbery took place. The only connection between the car and the robbery is that your father drove down from Leicester in it to meet Gerry."

Suddenly Rosso got up and walked to the door. The yard was empty and very quiet. "Where's Jason, Grandad?"

"I thought he was here with you."

"I hope nothing has happened to him. I think I'll take a look down the street, Grandad," said Rosso.

But there was no sign of the old dog anywhere.

Rosso usually slept very soundly, but that Saturday night he woke twice. The first time was because the telephone rang at about eleven o'clock. He could hear Jake talking to somebody. Then he heard Jake leave the caravan and start up the van. The second time Rosso woke was after midnight. He thought he could hear quiet noises outside the caravan. If Jason had been in the yard, of course, he would have barked. But Rosso suddenly remembered that Jason had disappeared.

He looked out of the window but could see nothing. Then he heard the noises again. They were coming from the garage where the Riley was kept. Somebody was in there, doing something to the car! Rosso got quietly out of bed and opened Jake's bedroom door. There was nobody there. Jake was not back yet – or perhaps he was outside in the garage, working. Rosso looked at his watch. 1 am! What would Jake be doing in the garage at 1 am?

And if it was not Jake in the garage, that meant that Jake had not come home! Where was he? The sensible thing to do, of course, would be to call the police, but Rosso (like many Romanies) did not trust the police much. So he quietly opened the door of the caravan and walked over to the garage. The door was shut but the light inside was on. Rosso peeped through a crack in the door and saw a very strange sight: two men were doing something to the Riley. The boot was open and the carpet was lying on the floor. The men had taken out the back seat, too. They had opened the front doors and were now pulling the inside door panels off the frames! As Rosso watched, he saw one man pull off the panel on the driver's side. Something made of metal fell out onto the floor and the man gave a cry of delight: "Here it is!"

"Where?"

"On the floor somewhere. It fell out of the door ..."

"Where is it?"

"It must be here somewhere. Come and help me look!"

But before the other man could move, the garage light went out. Rosso had pulled the master switch in the fuse-box beside the garage.

"What the hell?" cried one of the men.

"Get the torch, quick. It's in the car," and almost before Rosso could move to the side, the garage door was opened and somebody ran quietly past him across the yard.

There was a burglar alarm at the yard, but Jake rarely switched it on. The switch was in the fuse-box. Rosso waited until the man had reached the car before he moved the switch. The noise from the siren was enough to wake the dead. A few seconds later the second man was rushing past Rosso into the darkness of the yard towards the street, their car and safety. As soon as the burglars' car had turned the corner of Culvert Street, Rosso switched the alarm off, turned on the light again and ran into the garage.

Three minutes later he was back in the caravan with the thing which the two men had been looking for. It was an ordinary Yale key that looked as if it could belong to any of five million front doors in Britain. But Rosso knew – or thought he knew – what this key was: it would unlock the door of the place where half a million pounds in stolen bullion had been hidden. The kind of money that criminals might even kill for.

Then Rosso remembered that he was alone. Jake was not there and Jason was missing. Suddenly he felt afraid, and just as suddenly he knew that there was somebody else in the yard. He looked out of the window and saw the figure of a tall man standing in front of the open garage door. The man had switched the garage light on again, and his figure was only a shadow in the darkness outside the door, but Rosso knew him at once.

The man switched off the garage light, shut the doors and began walking slowly towards the caravan.

Chapter eight

Three missing persons

Julia was surprised to find that the gate to Jake's scrapyard was still locked when she arrived there on Sunday afternoon. She looked through a crack in the gate but there was no sign of Rosso. Jason was not sitting in his usual place, either, and the van was gone. So Jake must be out somewhere, too. She would come back later.

Just as she was walking away, a man who had been standing at the corner of the street came up to her. "Are you looking for somebody, Love?" he asked.

Julia did not like the look of the man. He was about fifty years old and was wearing a long raincoat. "No," she said. "I've lost my way. Can you tell me where Francis Chichester Way is?"

The man thought for a second, but it was obvious that he was a stranger to the area. "No," he said, "I don't know a street of that name in this part of London."

"Thank you," said Julia, and walked away.

She stopped when she reached the tunnel and looked back. The man was still watching her, but he did not follow. Julia walked a few steps down the tunnel, then turned around and walked carefully back to the tunnel entrance. She peeped round the corner. The man was standing in front of the gate, looking through a crack. What did he want? Where were Rosso and Jake? She began to feel worried.

There was nothing to do but walk home. Should she tell her mother? When she got back to the flat her mother said: *"Rosso hat vor einer Weile angerufen, Julia. Er wollte dich sprechen. Er ruft später nochmal an."*

"Oh! Schön!" At least nothing had happened to him, Julia thought. So she said nothing to her mother about the man at the scrapyard. Mr Witzkow was not in the flat. *"Wo ist Papa?"*

"Im Pub mit einigen Arbeitskollegen. Er kommt sicher bald nach Hause."

It seemed a long time before the phone in the Witzkows' flat rang and she heard Rosso's voice: "Is that you, Julia? Listen – I can't say much, I'm in a phone box, but there's something very important which I want you to do. Will you do it?"

"Of course, Rosso. What is it?"

"I need a key. It's in the yard. It's on top of the garage fuse-box."

"Fuse-box?" Julia repeated. She did not know the word.

"Yes, the wooden box on the wall to the left of the garage door. There's a Yale key – an ordinary door key – on top of the fuse-box. Can you bring it to me at Piccadilly Circus tonight? You know how to get here?"

"Number 19 bus?"

"Good girl!"

"But the yard gate is locked, Rosso. How can I get in?"

"You'll have to climb in – and out. Wear your oldest jeans and wait till it gets really dark. I'll meet you at the Eros statue at about eleven o'clock."

"All right, Rosso!" Julia was quite excited. What an adventure! "But where are you now? Where's Jake ...?"

There was no reply. Rosso had hung up.

"How long do you think you can keep me here before the police turn up?" asked Jake. He was lying on a low bed in the corner of a very strange room. It had no windows and a door at one end only. The ceiling was semicircular and made of brick. Every few minutes there was a low rumbling sound which got louder and louder until the whole room shook. Then the sound died away again.

Jake knew where he was. He was a prisoner in one of the arches under a railway line somewhere in south London. In front of the door sat a big man. He was reading a magazine and smoking a cigarette.

"Don't worry, Jake. As soon as we get the key we'll let you go. It's not his key, anyway. It belongs to Gerry, so he only wants what belongs to him. Just sit back and relax. Read a magazine or something until Gerry gets back with the key."

"You promise you won't hurt the boy?"

"Of course not. All we want is the key."

"What have you done with my dog?"

"Jason? He's all right. You'll get him back as soon as we've finished."

"Finished? Finished what?"

"Now then, Jake. Don't pretend you don't know all about it. Gerry spent nearly seven years in prison waiting for his chance to get his share of the loot. He's not going to stop until he's got it. He hid the key in your old Riley before they changed cars. Your son Raymond made sure that the police caught Gerry, but he himself escaped. Gerry just wants the gold – he doesn't want Raymond to go to prison, he doesn't want to hurt you, or the boy, or the dog, or the girl ..."

"The girl?"

"Yeah! Rosso's little German friend. Sid saw her looking for something down at your yard this morning. He thinks she knows where the key is. He's waiting there now with Gerry. As soon as we have the key, you can all go home."

Mr Witzkow came back from the pub at six o'clock. He looked worried. *"Wo ist Julia?"* he asked his wife.

"In ihrem Zimmer. Warum?"

"Schau dir diesen Artikel an! Ein Arbeitskollege hat ihn mir gezeigt!" It was the same article that Rosso had read. *"Der Mann, den die Polizei nicht erwischt hat, ist Raymond Smith, Rossos Vater! Jeder in der Kneipe weiß es! Wir sollten Julia den Umgang mit diesem Jungen verbieten. Ich spreche nach dem Abendessen mit ihr."*

Julia was quieter than usual during supper. She was thinking about her night adventure. Then suddenly she realized that her father was talking to her – about Rosso.

“ … deine Mutter und ich glauben nicht, dass du mit diesem Rosso soviel Zeit verbringen solltest. Er ist Zigeuner und sein Vater ein Verbrecher.”

“Das ist nicht wahr!” cried Julia. *“Ihr habt ihn beide kennengelernt und mit seinem Großvater gesprochen! Sie sind beide ganz normale Menschen – genauso wie wir! Wie könnt ihr bloß so intolerant sein!”*

Her father tried not to get angry. He just showed her the newspaper article. Julia read it in silence. She couldn’t believe that Rosso’s father was a criminal. She trusted Rosso and he trusted her. It just couldn’t be true!

Her mother put her arm round her shoulders and spoke to her in a quiet voice: *"Dein Vater meint es nur gut mit dir, Schatz! Ich mag Rosso auch sehr. Aber diese Sache mit dem Goldraub hat uns alle schockiert. Vielleicht solltest du dich mit Rosso nicht so oft treffen, bis sich der ganze Wirbel gelegt hat."*

But Julia was very angry now. *"Ich werde mich mit Rosso so oft treffen, wie ich will! Ich treffe mich mit ihm heute Abend ..."*

"Nein!" her father shouted. *"Du bleibst schön hier!"*

"Aber ich habe ihm versprochen, mich mit ihm am Piccadilly Circus zu treffen ..."

"Das tust du nicht! London ist eine gefährliche Großstadt, besonders bei Nacht. Wir möchten nicht, dass unserer einzigen Tochter etwas zustößt!"

Her father tried to talk to her quietly and in a friendly way, but Julia shouted back: *"Ihr habt mich hierhergeschleppt und jetzt, wo ich endlich einen richtigen Freund gefunden habe, verbietet ihr mir den Umgang mit ihm! Das ist einfach nicht fair!"*

Julia knew this was the wrong thing to say. Her parents had always been fair to her. But she had to find some way of meeting Rosso. She had promised. Mr Witzkow was very angry now.

"Jetzt gehst du in dein Zimmer, Julia, und kommst erst wieder, wenn du dich entschuldigen willst!"

Julia started to say something but changed her mind. It was no use arguing with her father. She walked out of the living-room and locked her bedroom door behind her.

There were several interesting programmes on TV that evening, and it was almost eleven o'clock when Mr Witzkow remembered that Julia was still in her room. He was sorry that he had shouted at her, so he went to her bedroom and knocked on the door. *"Julia – darf ich reinkommen?"* There was no answer. Mr Witzkow turned the door-knob, but the door was still locked on the inside. *"Mach bitte auf, Julia."* Still there was no reply.

"Sie schläft vielleicht schon," said his wife.

"Nein, das Licht brennt noch." He tried to look through the keyhole, but all he could see was the open bedroom window.

"Und das Fenster ist weit offen ..."

"Du glaubst doch nicht ...?"

"Komm mit!"

They ran out of the flat and down the stairs into the garden. Looking up, they saw that Julia's window on the second floor was, indeed, wide open. A rope of knotted bed-sheets was hanging out of the window. There was no sign of Julia.

"Wo wollte sie sich mit diesem Rosso treffen? Piccadilly Circus? Am besten, wir nehmen ein Taxi ..."

Chapter nine

Complications

At about the same time as Mr and Mrs Witzkow were getting into a taxi on their way to Piccadilly Circus, the tall man Rosso had met in the scrapyard the night before was sitting in a car and waiting for something to happen. It was just before eleven o'clock. From his car he could see Culvert Street, the tunnel and Culvert Place. Occasionally somebody walked past, but as far as the man could see there was nobody waiting in any of the dark doorways.

There was no sign of the girl yet. Rosso had said that she was going to meet him at Piccadilly Circus with the key at eleven. She would not have much time because there were not many buses in the late evening. He lit another French cigarette. Smoking was bad for him, he knew. But he was very nervous tonight. If things went wrong and the police caught him, he might go to prison for something he had never done.

Then at last he saw her – a small figure running quickly out of the tunnel and into Culvert Place. She ran up to the gate of the scrapyard and looked around once or twice before climbing over the wall.

One minute went by, then two. The man became even more nervous. What on earth was the girl doing all this time? It shouldn't take her as long as this to ... Then he suddenly thought: supposing somebody was waiting for Julia *inside* the yard? He had not thought of that. His plan was going wrong ...

And suddenly he saw the yard gates open wide. Seconds later, with a powerful roar and with all four headlights on, the Riley, his own beautiful limousine, drove quickly out of the yard, down Culvert Place, and turned left into Culvert Road. Sid Mulligan was driving and Gerry Smith was sitting on the back seat with the girl!

He started the car and followed the red tail-lights of the Riley into Versleigh Road and the streets of Europe's biggest city. He had an idea of where they were going but knew that he would have to phone the police very quickly if he wanted his plan to be successful. One thing he did not understand was why they had taken his car. Everybody in Battersea knew it ... Then he realized why. Of course! People would see it and remember it: Raymond Smith's car, found at the place where the bullion had been hidden for all these years. He would never be able to clear his name if that happened!

He stopped outside a phone box, ran in and dialled 999.

"Emergency – which service do you require?"

"Police – quick!"

"Lavender Hill Police Station."

"I wish to report a stolen car."

"This number is for emergencies only, for stolen cars ..."

"Listen! I haven't got much time! This car was stolen by Gerry Smith – the escaped bullion robber. Sid Mulligan is driving it. They've kidnapped a girl. They're on their way to the place where the rest of the loot from the bullion robbery is hidden. They're driving down Battersea Park Road towards Nine Elms now. The car is a 1950 Riley: red and cream with a black roof. You can't miss it. I've got an idea where the car is going. I expect it to stay south of the Thames, so you can concentrate on Camberwell and Bermondsey. Whatever you do, don't stop the car until they reach their destination. Have you got that? Please hurry! I expect your people would like a word with me, too! You've been looking for me for nearly seven years. I'm Raymond Smith."

Rosso looked at his watch for the fifth time in five minutes. It was already twenty past eleven. Julia was late. He wondered if anything had happened to her. No. Dad would be there to look after her, of course. Although Rosso had had less than twenty-four hours to find out what kind of a man his father was, he trusted him. Everything would be all right now that Dad was back! Dad would make everything right.

"Where's our daughter? Where's Julia?!"

Mr Witzkow had recognized Rosso and grabbed him by the shoulder.

"Oh! Hello, Mr Witzkow. Julia ...?"

"Yes! She said she was meeting you here – she climbed out of her bedroom window to come here! She could have broken her neck! Our only daughter! *Zigeunerpack!*"

Rosso didn't know what the last word meant – luckily – but he didn't like the sound of it. He could see that Mr Witzkow was very angry, so he tried to explain: "I'm waiting here for Julia, but she's late. Two number 19 buses have come by but she wasn't on either of them. Let's wait for the next one ..."

"No. Julia is only fifteen and it's nearly midnight. She's missing from home. This is a case for the police." And as if by magic a young police constable who had been watching them suddenly walked up.

"Is there anything wrong, sir? Can I help?"

"Yes, our daughter Julia is missing ..."

"Don't worry, Love," said the man who was driving the Riley. "All we want is the key. As soon as we're sure it's the right one, we'll let you go."

Julia said nothing. She had given them the key. They were driving far too fast, and there were no seat-belts in the old car.

"Slow down, Sid!" growled the big man sitting next to her. "We'll be stopped for speeding!"

Sid slowed down a bit, but he was still driving too fast.

"Where are you taking me?" asked Julia.

"To see your friend Jake. It's not far now. We'll soon be there."

Julia thought about Rosso, who would be waiting for her at Piccadilly Circus. What could she do?

"Stop the car please!" she said. "I feel sick!" But the big man just opened the window, pointed to it and smiled.

"Go ahead! But don't fall out, and don't be sick all over the seats! They're real leather!"

Julia sat back. It was no good. She would have to wait and see where they were taking her. The car turned left off the main road. The street-lights were not so bright here. The houses were smaller and older. Some of them were almost in ruins. They turned right into an even smaller side-street, and Julia saw in front of the car, in the light of the headlights, a high brick wall with a metal railing along the top. Then she saw that the brick wall was really a line of railway arches closed in with wooden walls in which there were no windows, only doors or gates.

"Here we are," said Sid. "It's Arch Number Two."

Chapter ten

Chase through the night

The sergeant at the police station was very friendly. He listened to both sides of the story, but he could not help them. "Perhaps Julia is waiting for you at Piccadilly Circus now," he said to Rosso. "Or perhaps she has gone back to your flat in Battersea," he said to the Witzkows. "It's not quite midnight, and she isn't really a missing person yet ..."

Finally Rosso told him who he was and all about his father's plan to catch the bullion thieves. The sergeant stopped smiling. This was serious! He went into his office and phoned Scotland Yard. He dialled the Witzkows' number, but there was no reply. Then he went back to the main office where Rosso and Julia's parents were waiting.

"I must ask you to wait here, young man," he said to Rosso. Then he turned to the Witzkows and said: "The best thing would be for you to go home and wait for your daughter there."

"But I don't want to go home!" cried Mrs Witzkow. "Where is our daughter? What has happened to her?"

"Please try and keep calm," said the sergeant. "This is a police matter and we can't involve the general public."

"But we're not the general public!" said Mrs Witzkow. "We're Julia's parents, and Rosso's father is out there somewhere, too. We're already involved ..."

Just as the sergeant was going to say something, a plain-clothes inspector walked into the room. He talked quietly to the sergeant before turning to the other three. "Mr and Mrs Witzkow? Rosso? I'm Inspector Darrow from Scotland Yard. We think it would be a good idea if you came with us." He led them outside into a big black police car. "Camberwell Green, as fast as you can!" he said to the driver, and the car drove off into the night with blue lights flashing and siren wailing.

"Please tell us what's happening, sir," said Rosso.

"I'll tell you what I know, young man. Then I might need your help. We had a phone call from your father about a stolen car. Two of the bullion robbers have stolen his old Riley and he thinks that they are on their way to the place where the rest of the bullion is hidden. We're sure that the car hasn't come north of the River Thames, but we're not quite sure where they are now. You know the car, and probably the registration number too."

"Of course. It's 2380 PK. I'd know the car anywhere. I don't know where the bullion is, but I think I've got the key."

"What?! You mean they've kidnapped the girl and she doesn't even have the right key! This is serious!"

The police car was already crossing Westminster Bridge. The streets were still quite busy although it was almost midnight, and cars, buses and vans all had to stop to let the big police car past.

"Serious? What do you mean?" asked Julia's mother. "Is our daughter in any danger?"

"If the robbers think they've been tricked, Julia may be in danger," said the inspector. "We must find them before that happens. Any news on the radio, Simmons?"

"Not yet, sir. But the other cars are closing in. They can't escape."

"All right. Stop here. We'll wait. Let's hope your father phones again soon, Rosso!"

Ray had been right. The Riley was parked in a side street beside the railway arches. Old memories came back to him. Arch Number Two had been Jake's workshop before he had bought the yard in Culvert Place. And then he remembered something else. There used to be a phone box just around the next corner. No sign of any police cars yet. Perhaps he should ring again. He got out of the car and walked around the corner. The old red phone box was still there.

He was just picking up the phone when he heard a dog bark. The sound was very close but weak – as if the dog were in a wooden box, or a car boot! Ray listened again, and again he heard the bark. It was coming from a car that was parked opposite the phone box. Someone had locked a dog in the boot! Nothing made Ray angrier than cruelty to animals. People who locked dogs in car boots should be locked up in small, dark boxes for a few hours! He ran across to the car and tried the boot – it was not locked. He carefully opened it and, to his amazement, found himself staring at his father's dog Jason.

Jason had been drugged and was just waking up. Ray stroked the old dog and whispered a few words in his ear. Then he helped Jason out of the boot and quietly closed it.

The pieces of the jigsaw puzzle were slowly coming together. Gerry and his friends must have drugged Jason and kidnapped Jake before they had broken into the garage to look for the key. Jake could not be far away. Kidnapping was a serious crime, and Ray smiled to himself. But he would only be happy when Jake and Julia were both safe.

He took Jason into the phone box with him and dialled 999 again.

"Message from headquarters, sir," said the driver of the police car. "Smith has just phoned again. The stolen car is parked outside the railway arches in Enid Street, Bermondsey, not far from London Bridge Station. But Smith says he doesn't think the bullion is hidden there."

"How on earth can he know that?" asked the inspector.

"He says the girl and one of the men are still outside in the car. Only the other man has gone in. Smith thinks his father may be in there."

"Grandad must be in there!" cried Rosso. "He can't be anywhere else."

"The dog is safe, too," said the driver.

"Never mind the dog," growled Inspector Darrow, who did not like animals much. "We'll give them five minutes. If they don't move, we'll have to get closer, just in case. If they do move, we'll follow them!"

"The girl has given us the key. You stay here with Jake," said Gerry. "We'll take the girl with us. We'll phone you when it's safe to let the old man go."

"OK, Boss. Good luck!"

"We won't need luck!" said Gerry. But he was wrong.

Ray watched him walk out of the door of Arch Number Two and get into the Riley. Jason began to growl when he saw Gerry. Sid, who had been sitting in the back with Julia, got into the driver's seat, started the car and drove off. Ray wanted to follow them, but he could not leave his father as a hostage. The police could chase Gerry – he would rescue Jake.

He crossed the street with Jason, who had now woken up fully, and stood outside the door of the arch. Jason sniffed and began to whine – he knew that Jake was inside. Suddenly Ray had his best idea of the day.

He tried the door – it was not locked, so he pushed the door open a little and let the dog in.

There was a loud bark, a surprised cry from the man who was guarding Jake, and a shout of delight from Jake himself. One hostage was free. Now they only had to worry about Julia.

"They're moving!" said Simmons. "They're turning right under the railway lines into Jamaica Road. It looks as if they might be heading for the Rotherhithe Tunnel."

"The Rotherhithe Tunnel? That would take them north of the Thames – out of their own territory."

"Territory?" asked Mr Witzkow.

"London crooks usually stay on their own side of the river," the inspector explained. "Gerry and his gang worked south of the Thames. If they hid the loot north of the Thames they were taking a big risk. Have we got a car waiting at the north end of the tunnel, Simmons?"

"Not yet, sir."

"Well, we'd better organize one! And we'd better follow them in ourselves, just to be on the safe side."

While Simmons drove quickly through the almost empty streets of Bermondsey, Inspector Darrow radioed for a car to wait at the north end of the Rotherhithe Tunnel. It was all very exciting. Rosso almost forgot that Julia was still a hostage.

They turned into Jamaica Road and Rosso gave a shout: "There they are!" There was only one car in the street, and although it was four hundred yards ahead of them there could be no mistake. It was the Riley.

"Slow down a bit, Simmons!" said the inspector. "They mustn't see us!"

"They're certainly going into the tunnel, sir," said the driver. But before the police car could follow them in, the inspector had to stop and radio the car at the north end of the tunnel. The radio would not work underground, of course, and they had to be sure the police car was waiting.

"Hello Alpha Charlie," said Darrow. "Please identify yourselves and give your present position."

"We're in a dark blue Ford Escort and we're still waiting at the north exit of the tunnel. No sign of your Riley yet."

"That's strange! They should have reached you by now. Are you sure?"

"No car like the one you described has been past yet."

"Well, we can't wait all night. They'll be with you in a moment or two. We're coming through now. Over and out."

The Rotherhithe Tunnel is a mile and a quarter long and is lit from end to end by bright lights. There is only one tunnel for both directions, so it is impossible to 'lose' a car in it, and nobody in Inspector Darrow's car saw another car as they drove through. When they reached the other end, Constable Simmons suddenly put the brakes full on and the heavy police car slid to a sudden stop.

"What now?" growled Darrow angrily.

Simmons just pointed to the mirror and said: "That's our car, sir. Dark blue Ford Escort parked on the hard shoulder just outside the tunnel. They're still waiting. We must have lost the Riley before we came into the tunnel."

"We can't have!" cried Darrow as Simmons backed towards the other police car, "We saw them drive in! We can't have lost them!" But he knew Simmons must be right.

"Stop here, quick!" Gerry shouted to the driver. They were in the middle of the tunnel and there were no other cars in sight. "Now back into that opening behind us and turn off all the lights."

At the half-way point in the tunnel there was a short side tunnel for service vehicles with small rooms and cupboards in the tunnel wall for repair equipment. It was in one of these small rooms, seven years before, that Gerry, who had worked as an engineer in the tunnel, had hidden his half of the bullion. It was a very small room right at the back of the service tunnel, and had not been used for many years. Nobody had realized that the key was missing. Only Gerry had known where that key was: for seven years it had been hidden in the door of Ray Smith's Riley.

Gerry could, of course, have broken into the room without the key, but there would have been a risk of somebody seeing or hearing him. It would be quicker and more fun this way: he could revenge himself on his cousin Ray by using his car. Yes, this was much more exciting!

"Everybody out! But hold onto the girl!"

As she got out, Julia saw that there was another car behind them in the service tunnel – not a car, in fact, but a small van. Then she realized that it was Jake's old Ford van. A man got out of the van and walked towards Gerry.

Gerry walked back to the last door and took the key out of his pocket.

"Car coming!" shouted Sid who was watching the road from the end of the service tunnel. "Looks like the police!"

It was. The big black police car drove quickly past, but Inspector Darrow and Constable Simmons had no idea that they were in fact driving past the car they were 'following'. Everybody stood perfectly still. Sid held Julia's arm even more tightly, but he had no idea that Julia had done a little judo at her sports club in Angermünde. Her judo teacher had shown her one or two tricks. She hoped this one would work. She made a quick movement forwards. Sid tried to pull her back. As quick as lightning she changed direction and Sid fell backwards, hitting his head on the tunnel wall.

Julia just ran. The second hostage was free.

"Quick, boss! The girl is escaping!" cried Sid.

"Never mind the girl! She's got half a mile to run in either direction, and the police must be miles away by now! We've got the key, come on! We've got to be quick!"

He smiled as he pushed the key into the keyhole.

It was Rosso who heard Julia's whistle first. Far away down the tunnel and very faint, but there could be no mistake. It was the special Romany whistle he had given her. He had never thought she would need it, and he had no idea that she had carried it on a string around her neck ever since he had given it to her.

"Listen!" he cried, breaking into the angry conversation between the inspector and the other policemen. "It's Julia!"

The others listened but it was several seconds before their ears caught the faint sound above the silence of the night.

"Are you sure?" asked the inspector.

"Of course I am! She's down there in the tunnel! Come on!" and before anyone could stop him he was running back down into the tunnel. Inspector Darrow only waited a few seconds to give instructions to his men before turning the car round and following Rosso.

All three met at a point about a quarter of a mile inside the tunnel. The Inspector could not be sure, but he thought Rosso must have run the distance in almost Olympic time.

Julia's whistle had told them that Gerry and the others were still in the tunnel, and more police cars were now moving quickly down it from both ends. Inspector Darrow stopped to pick up Julia and Rosso, then they drove on. They stopped just in front of the service tunnel where Gerry was still struggling to break open the locked door with a heavy crowbar. The useless key which Julia had given him was lying forgotten on the ground beside him.

"Stay in the car, you two!" said Inspector Darrow, but neither Rosso nor Julia had any intention of staying in the car. They were following him towards the service tunnel entrance when a voice which Rosso was beginning to recognize well shouted: "Rosso! Come here!"

It was his father.

Ray Smith got out of the first police car which had come up the tunnel from the south side. He ran over to his son. Mr and Mrs Witzkow arrived at about the same time in the dark blue Ford.

Nobody spoke. They just watched as Gerry, Sid and the other man were put into police cars.

Inspector Darrow held out his hand and Rosso gave him the key which he had had in his jeans pocket all the time.

Darrow walked down the service tunnel, past the Riley and Jake's blue van to the last door and opened it. Inside were four metal boxes. Inside each box, they knew, was over £100,000 in gold and platinum bars. The inspector looked first at the boxes, then at Ray.

Then in his most formal policeman's voice – the voice he used when arresting criminals – he said: "Raymond George Smith?"

"Yes, Inspector."

"It is my duty to warn you that … that if you don't move that old car of yours and follow us down to the police station in it, I will have to arrest you for … for … for illegal parking in the Rotherhithe Tunnel!"

Everybody laughed – even Raymond.

CHAPTER ELEVEN

All's well that ends well

"So the only way to clear my name was to find out where the bullion had been hidden and tell the police where it was," said Ray later at the police station. "Only Gerry knew that, and he would not tell anyone until he was safely out of prison. As soon as I heard that he had escaped, I knew that I would have to find him before he could get to the rest of the bullion. When Sid Mulligan came to the yard and tried to buy my car, I was sure that Gerry had hidden something – perhaps a key – in the Riley when we had met at the motorway service area. But Jake wouldn't sell the car, of course. Then Gerry asked somebody to phone Jake with some story about finding his dog. Jake drove to the place where he thought Jason had been found but was kidnapped and taken to Arch Number Two. Gerry sent two of his friends to steal the car. But Rosso had taken out the rotor arm, so they couldn't drive it away. Only Gerry knew exactly where the key was, and he didn't trust his friends. He wanted the car in one piece. But when the two burglars realized that they couldn't steal the car, they had to take it apart on the spot and look for the key. That's when Rosso caught them.

"I had followed them, but they didn't see me – luckily. When I knew that Rosso had the key they were looking for, I realized that they would come back for it. It was too soon to call the police. I wanted to catch them red-handed. If they thought they had the right key, they would go to the place where the loot was hidden. But they had Jake and Jason, so we had to be careful.

"My first plan was to post them the key in the hope that they would ask no questions. When Rosso told me that Sid Mulligan had seen Julia near the yard, I arranged for Rosso to ask Julia to fetch something important from the caravan – a key. If anyone was watching the yard, they would see her go in and come out with something."

"But suppose something had happened to Julia?" asked Mrs Witzkow.

"Yes. I'm sorry about that, Mrs Witzkow. It was my mistake, but it was a risk I had to take. I shouldn't have put the rotor arm back. But I never thought they would take the car, and I was only a few yards from the gate," said Ray. "I could easily have handled Sid if he had tried to take Julia hostage instead of just taking the key off her – he's fifteen years older than me! The rest you know. My plan started to go wrong when they drove off in the Riley. I followed them. Then I phoned the police. The police followed me to Arch Number Two, where we rescued Jake with Jason's help. Then I followed you to the tunnel in a police car. Is there anything else you'd like to know?"

"Yes," said Rosso, rather stiffly. "Why didn't you write, or phone, or tell me where you were all these years?"

There was a moment's silence before Ray went on: "If the bullion robbers or the police had known where I was – or that you knew how to contact me, Rosso – neither you, nor Jake, nor your mother would have had a moment's peace all these years. You know what people think about us gypsies – crooks, all of us! It was my bad luck that I went to help Gerry that night and that he hid the key in my car. When we drove off in his car, I had no idea what he had done ... he didn't tell me about the bullion robbery until the police started following us! By then it was too late. He said he would tell the police I was an accomplice. He made me drive faster!"

"But why didn't he just tell somebody where the key was?" asked Julia. "Why wait seven years?"

"He didn't trust anyone else to fetch the key – he wanted to do that himself. And he never forgave me for crashing his Aston Martin. It was beautiful – a real James Bond car! Beautiful but thirsty! The police only caught us because we ran out of petrol! I drove the car into the side of a bridge – Gerry was on the passenger's side and couldn't get out because he couldn't open the door. I got out and ran. I only stopped running last week when I heard that Gerry had escaped."

"You don't think much of police efficiency, Mr Smith," said the inspector, rather stiffly.

"The risk was too great, Inspector. The key was hidden in my car, Gerry was my cousin. We were all in the same boat. I had no choice – or did I?"

There was more silence before Inspector Darrow said: "No. Perhaps you didn't. But things might have been easier for everybody if you hadn't run away."

"Maybe, but it's too late to worry about that now," said Ray. "I've wasted seven years of my life – your life, too, Rosso – on the run. That's punishment enough." Then he asked the question that was worrying him most: "Will there be any criminal charges made against me, Inspector?"

"I can't say at the moment, Mr Smith. But I shouldn't think so. You've helped us to recover the bullion – there might even be a small reward from the insurance company. We'll need your evidence at the trial, of course."

"Of course, Inspector. You'll know where to find me." He put his arm round Rosso's shoulders. "I won't be far from Culvert Place from now on!"

When he heard his home mentioned, Jason suddenly gave a loud bark.

"Good old Jason!" cried Jake. "We almost forgot you!"

"He'll be all right now, won't he?" asked Julia, who was beginning to develop an almost English love for animals.

"Yes, but he's an old dog, Julia. We mustn't expect him to live for ever. This has been the adventure of his life!"

"Then everything's OK. 'All's well that ends well'," said Julia happily. "Shakespeare – I mean: Mrs Pyne's private English lessons!"

And for the second time that night everybody began to laugh.

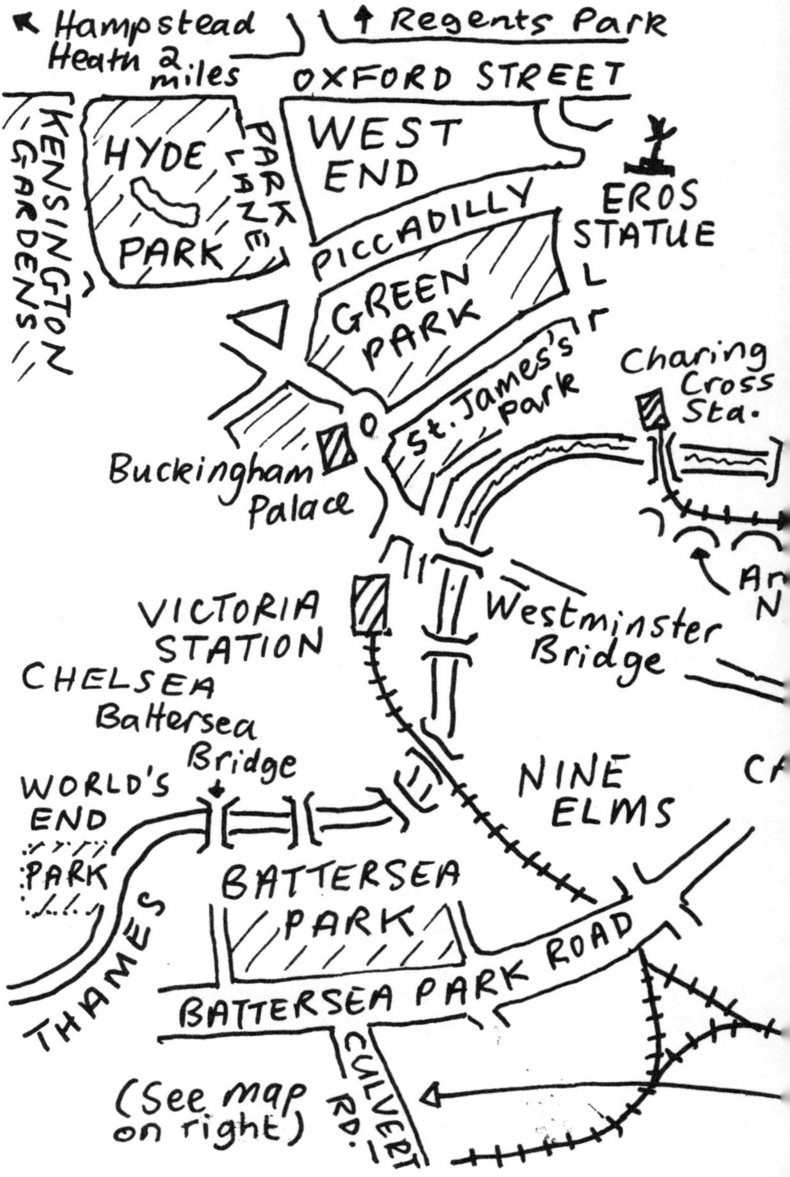
Hampstead Heath 2 miles
Regents Park
OXFORD STREET
KENSINGTON GARDENS
HYDE PARK
PARK LANE
WEST END
EROS STATUE
PICCADILLY
GREEN PARK
St. James's Park
Charing Cross Sta.
Buckingham Palace
VICTORIA STATION
Westminster Bridge
CHELSEA
Battersea Bridge
WORLD'S END
PARK
NINE ELMS
BATTERSEA PARK
THAMES
BATTERSEA PARK ROAD
CULVERT RD.
(See map on right)

ROSSO and JULIA'S LONDON

This is a page from Rosso's diary. It shows most of the places in the story.

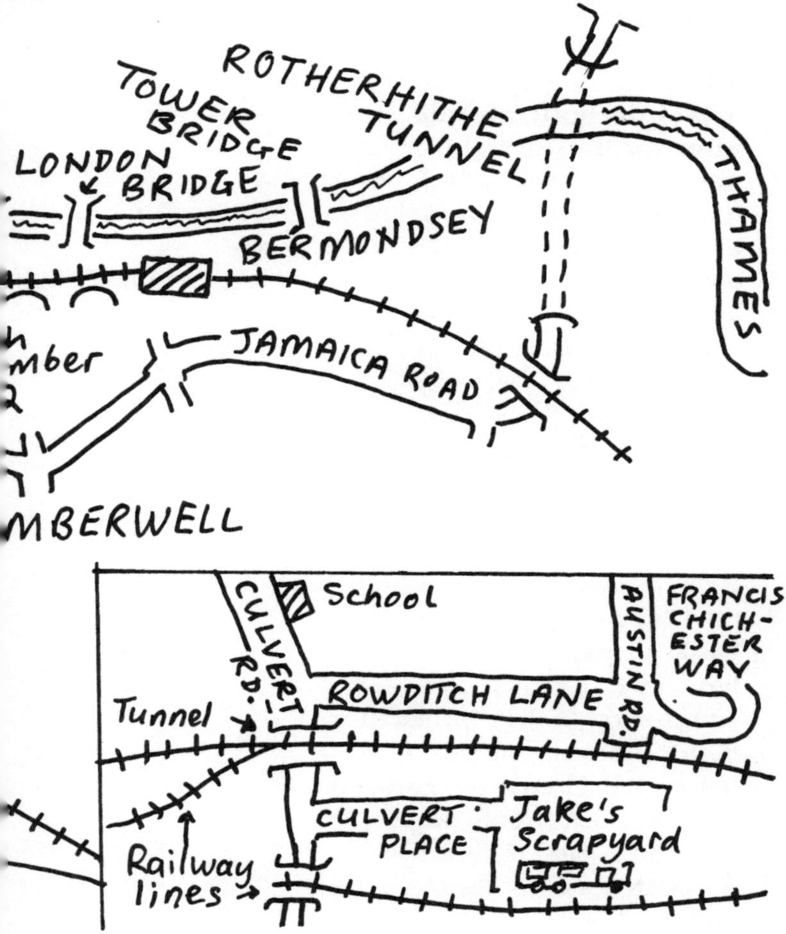

Vocabulary

pl. = plural, *n.* = noun, *sb.* = somebody, *sth.* = something, *BE* = British English, *infml.* = informal

A **accomplice** [ə'kʌmplɪs] Komplize/Komplizin
across [ə'krɒs] hinüber
action: out of action ['ækʃn] außer Betrieb, nicht einsatzfähig
affair [ə'feə] Angelegenheit
afraid: (to) **be/feel afraid** [ə'freɪd] Angst haben
afterwards ['ɑːftəwədz] danach
ahead of sb./sth. [ə'hed] vor jm./etw.
(to) **allow sb. sth.** [ə'laʊ] jm. etw. erlauben
alsatian (dog) [æl'seɪʃn] Schäferhund
amazement [ə'meɪzmənt] Verwunderung, Erstaunen
apart [ə'pɑːt] auseinander
arch [ɑːtʃ] Gewölbe
armed [ɑːmd] bewaffnet
(to) **arrange** [ə'reɪndʒ] arrangieren
(to) **arrest** [ə'rest] verhaften
(to) **associate** [ə'səʊʃieɪt] in Verbindung bringen
awkward ['ɔːkwəd] verlegen

B (to) **back** [bæk] zurückfahren
bank [bæŋk] Ufer
bar [bɑː] Barren
bed-sheet ['bedʃiːt] Bettlaken
beside [bɪ'saɪd] neben
better: we'd better organize one wir sollten besser/lieber einen organisieren
bit: a bit [bɪt] ein bisschen
(to) **bite** [baɪt] beißen
blond [blɒnd] blond

blood: (to) **be after sb.'s blood** [blʌd] jm. an den Kragen wollen
boot *(BE)* [buːt] Kofferraum
breath: (to) **take a deep breath** [breθ] einmal tief Luft holen
brick [brɪk] Backstein, Ziegelstein
bullion ['bʊliən] (Gold-, Platin-, Silber-)Barren
(to) **bump into sb.** [bʌmp] mit jm. zusammenstoßen
bunch [bʌntʃ] Strauß
burglar ['bɜːglə] Einbrecher/in
burglar alarm ['bɜːglər‿əˌlɑːm] Alarmanlage

C **cafeteria** [ˌkæfə'tɪəriə] *hier:* Mensa
calm [kɑːm] ruhig
carved [kɑːvd] geschnitzt
case [keɪs] Fall
case: just in case nur für den Fall
(to) **catch sb. red-handed** [ˌred'hændɪd] jn. auf frischer Tat ertappen
(to) **catch up with sb.** [ˌkætʃ‿'ʌp] jn. einholen
chase [tʃeɪs] Verfolgungsjagd
(to) **chase** [tʃeɪs] jagen, verfolgen
choice [tʃɔɪs] Wahl
chrome [krəʊm] Chrom
cigarette [ˌsɪgə'ret] Zigarette
circus ['sɜːkəs] Zirkus
classy ['klɑːsi] nobel
(to) **clear one's name** [klɪə] seine Unschuld beweisen
close [kləʊs] nahe
(to) **close in sb.** [ˌkləʊz‿'ɪn] jn. umzingeln
closed in with „dichtgemacht" mit
(to) **come by** [ˌkʌm 'baɪ] vorbeikommen
(to) **come round** [ˌkʌm 'raʊnd] vorbeikommen

complication [ˌkɒmplɪˈkeɪʃn] Komplikation
(to) **concentrate on** [ˈkɒnsntreɪt] (sich) konzentrieren auf
connection [kəˈnekʃn] Zusammenhang
constable [ˈkʌnstəbl] Polizist
(to) **contact** [ˈkɒntækt] erreichen
convenient [kənˈviːniənt] günstig
couple [ˈkʌpl] Paar
crack *(n.)* [kræk] Riss, Ritze
(to) **crash** [kræʃ] kaputtfahren
crime [kraɪm] Verbrechen
crook [krʊk] Gauner/in
crowbar [ˈkrəʊbɑː] Brecheisen
cruelty [ˈkruːəlti] Grausamkeit, Quälerei
cry *(n.)* [kraɪ] Schrei

D **darkness** [ˈdɑːknəs] Dunkelheit
dark-haired [ˌdɑːkˈheəd] dunkelhaarig
delight [dɪˈlaɪt] Freude
(to) **deserve** [dɪˈzɜːv] verdienen
destination [ˌdestɪˈneɪʃn] Ziel
(to) **develop** [dɪˈveləp] entwickeln
(to) **dial** [ˈdaɪəl] wählen
(to) **die away** [ˌdaɪ‿əˈweɪ] leiser werden
direction [dəˈrekʃn] Richtung
(to) **disappear** [ˌdɪsəˈpɪə] verschwinden
distance [ˈdɪstəns] Strecke
do: ... and so did Rosso und Rosso auch
door-knob [ˈdɔːnɒb] Türknauf
doorway [ˈdɔːweɪ] Eingang
(to) **drug** [drʌg] betäuben
duck [dʌk] Ente
duty [ˈdjuːti] Pflicht

E **earth: How/What on earth ...?** [ɜːθ] Wie/Was in aller Welt ...?
efficiency [ɪ'fɪʃnsi] Fähigkeit
either: she wasn't on either of them sie war in keinem der beiden (Busse)
emergency [i'mɜːdʒənsi] *etwa:* Notrufzentrale, Einsatzzentrale
entrance ['entrəns] Eingang
equipment [ɪ'kwɪpmənt] *hier:* Geräte
escape *(n.)* [ɪ'skeɪp] Flucht
ever since [ˌevə 'sɪns] seither, seitdem
evidence ['evɪdəns] Aussage
exactly [ɪg'zæktli] genau
exit ['eksɪt] Ausgang
exotic [ɪg'zɒtɪk] exotisch
(to) **explore** [ɪk'splɔː] erkunden

F **faint** [feɪnt] schwach
familiar [fə'mɪliə] bekannt
fascinated: (to) **be fascinated** ['fæsɪneɪtɪd] fasziniert sein
fault [fɔːlt] Schuld
filling-station ['fɪlɪŋˌsteɪʃn] Tankstelle
flamingo, *pl.:* **flamingos** [flə'mɪŋgəʊ, -z] Flamingo
(to) **flash** [flæʃ] blinken
floor [flɔː] Etage
(to) **forgive** [fə'gɪv] verzeihen
formal ['fɔːml] förmlich, offiziell
forwards ['fɔːwədz] nach vorne
frame *(n.)* [freɪm] Rahmen
friendship ['frendʃɪp] Freundschaft
fuse-box ['fjuːzbɒks] Sicherungskasten

G (to) **gallop** ['gæləp] galoppieren
gang [gæŋ] Bande
general public [ˌdʒenrəl 'pʌblɪk] Öffentlichkeit
generation [ˌdʒenə'reɪʃn] Generation
(to) **get sth.** *hier:* etw. verstehen
(to) **go wrong** [ˌgəʊ 'rɒŋ] schief gehen
good: It was no good. Es nützte nichts.
(to) **grab** [græb] packen
grandad ['grændæd] Großvater
grandson ['grænsʌn] Enkel
(to) **grass on sb.** [grɑːs] jn. verpfeifen
(to) **grow up** [ˌgrəʊ‿'ʌp] erwachsen werden
(to) **growl** [graʊl] knurren
(to) **guard** [gɑːd] bewachen
guilty ['gɪlti] schuldig
gypsy ['dʒɪpsi] Zigeuner/in

H **halfway** [ˌhɑːf'weɪ] halb
handicrafts ['hændikrɑːfts] Werken, Werkunterricht
(to) **handle** ['hændl] fertig werden mit
(to) **hang up** [ˌhæŋ‿'ʌp] auflegen
hard shoulder [ˌhɑːd 'ʃəʊldə] Seitenstreifen
harm: (to) **do harm to sb.** [hɑːm] jm. Schaden zufügen
have got to (tun) müssen
(to) **head for** [hed] fahren in Richtung
headlights ['hedlaɪts] Scheinwerfer
headline ['hedlaɪn] Schlagzeile
headquarters [ˌhed'kwɔːtəz] (Polizei-)Präsidium
hell: What the hell ...? [hel] Verdammt noch mal!
(to) **hold onto** [ˌhəʊld‿'ɒntə] festhalten
(to) **hold out one's hand** [ˌhəʊld‿'aʊt] die Hand ausstrecken
hold-up ['həʊldʌp] bewaffneter Raubüberfall

hostage ['hɒstɪdʒ] Geisel
houseboat ['haʊsbəʊt] Hausboot

I (to) **identify** [aɪ'dentɪfaɪ] *wörtlich:* sich identifizieren, *hier:* sich zu erkennen geben
illegal [ɪ'li:gl] unerlaubt
impossible [ɪm'pɒsəbl] unmöglich
indeed [ɪn'di:d] tatsächlich
instead of [ɪn'sted] anstatt
instruction [ɪn'strʌkʃn] Anweisung
insurance [ɪn'ʃʊərəns] Versicherung
intention [ɪn'tenʃn] Absicht
involved: (to) **be involved in** [ɪn'vɒlvd] beteiligt sein an
It was no good. Es nützte nichts.
Italian [ɪ'tæliən] italienisch; Italienisch

J **jealous** ['dʒeləs] neidisch, eifersüchtig
jigsaw puzzle ['dʒɪgsɔ: ˌpʌzl] Puzzle
(to) **join** [dʒɔɪn] sich anschließen

K (to) **keep a diary** ['daɪəri] (ein) Tagebuch führen
(to) **keep doing sth.** etw. dauernd tun
keyhole ['ki:həʊl] Schlüsselloch
kid [kɪd] Kind
(to) **kidnap** ['kɪdnæp] entführen
knotted ['nɒtɪd] verknotet

L **leather** ['leðə] Leder
lie *(n.)* [laɪ] Lüge
(to) **lie, lied, lied** [laɪ, laɪd, laɪd] lügen

(to) **lie to sb.** [laɪ] jn. anlügen
lightning ['laɪtnɪŋ] Blitz
limousine ['lɪməziːn, ˌlɪmə'ziːn] Limousine
lit: (to) **light, lit, lit** [laɪt, lɪt, lɪt] *or* **lighted, lighted** ['laɪtɪd, 'laɪtɪd] beleuchten; anzünden
little ['lɪtl] wenig
local ['ləʊkl] lokal
look: (to) **have/take a look at sth.** sich etw. ansehen
look: I don't like the look of him. Er gefällt mir gar nicht.
loot [luːt] Beute
(to) **lose one's way** [ˌluːz wʌnz 'weɪ] sich verlaufen
Love mein/e Liebe/r
luck: bad luck [ˌbæd 'lʌk] Pech
luck: Good luck! [ˌgʊd 'lʌk] Viel Glück!
luckily ['lʌkɪli] glücklicherweise
lumbago [lʌm'beɪgəʊ] Hexenschuss

M (to) **make sb. do sth.** jn. zu etw. bringen/zwingen
(to) **make sb. laugh** jn. zum Lachen bringen
(to) **make (criminal) charges against sb.** [ˌkrɪmɪnl 'tʃɑːdʒɪz] gegen jn. Anklage erheben
(to) **make friends with sb.** sich mit jm. anfreunden
(to) **make sure** [ˌmeɪk 'ʃʊə, ˌmeɪk 'ʃɔː] darauf achten
master switch ['mɑːstə swɪtʃ] Hauptschalter
matter *(n.)* ['mætə] Sache, Angelegenheit
maybe ['meɪbi] vielleicht
memory ['meməri] Erinnerung
(to) **mention** ['menʃn] erwähnen
metal ['metl] Metall
metalwork ['metəlwɜːk] Werken mit Metall
mind: (to) **change one's mind** [maɪnd] es sich anders überlegen

mind: Never mind the dog! Der Hund ist doch jetzt egal!
(to) **miss** [mɪs] verpassen, verfehlen
missing person [ˌmɪsɪŋ ˈpɜːsn] Vermisste/r
movement [ˈmuːvmənt] Bewegung

N **neither … nor** [ˈnaɪðə … nɔː] weder … noch
nickname [ˈnɪkneɪm] Spitzname
(to) **nod** [nɒd] nicken
none [nʌn] keine(r,s)
notebook [ˈnəʊtbʊk] Notizbuch
nowhere [ˈnəʊweə] nirgendwo

O **occasionally** [əˈkeɪʒnəli] hin und wieder
one by one [ˌwʌn baɪ ˈwʌn] eine(r,s) nach dem/der/dem anderen
opening [ˈəʊpnɪŋ] Lücke, Öffnung
ordinary [ˈɔːdnri] gewöhnlich
outsider [ˌaʊtˈsaɪdə] Außenseiter/in
over: (to) **be over** vorbei sein
Over and out. Ende.
(to) **own** [əʊn] besitzen

P (to) **paint** [peɪnt] bemalen, streichen
panel [ˈpænl] Verkleidung
PE [ˌpiː‿ˈiː] Turnen, Sport(unterricht)
(to) **peep** [piːp] gucken
perfectly [ˈpɜːfɪktli] völlig
phone box [ˈfəʊn bɒks] Telefonzelle
(to) **pick up the phone** den Telefonhörer abheben
plain-clothes inspector [ˌpleɪnkləʊðz‿ɪnˈspektə] Kripobeamte/r (in Zivil)

platinum ['plætɪnəm] Platin
playground ['pleɪgraʊnd] *hier:* Schulhof
pleased: (to) **be pleased** [pli:zd] sich freuen
plenty of ['plenti] viel
point *(n.)* [pɔɪnt] Stelle
(to) **point to** [pɔɪnt] zeigen auf
(to) **polish** ['pɒlɪʃ] polieren
position [pə'zɪʃn] Standort, Position
(to) **post** [pəʊst] mit der Post schicken
present ['preznt] derzeitig
(to) **pretend** [prɪ'tend] so tun, als ob
promise *(n.)* ['prɒmɪs] Versprechen
punishment ['pʌnɪʃmənt] Strafe
(to) **put the brakes full on** [breɪks] eine Vollbremsung machen

Q **quid** *(infml.)* [kwɪd] Pfund

R **radio** *(n.)* ['reɪdiəʊ] Funk
(to) **radio for a car** ['reɪdiəʊ] über Funk einen Wagen anfordern
railing ['reɪlɪŋ] Geländer
railway line ['reɪlweɪ laɪn] Gleis, Bahnlinie
raincoat ['reɪnkəʊt] Regenmantel
rarely ['reəli] selten
rather ['rɑ:ðə] ziemlich
(to) **realize** ['ri:əlaɪz] erkennen, sich bewusst werden
(to) **recover** [rɪ'kʌvə] wiederbekommen
registration number [ˌredʒɪ'streɪʃn ˌnʌmbə] Kraftfahrzeugkennzeichen
remission for good conduct [rɪ'mɪʃn, 'kɒndʌkt] Straferlass wegen guter Führung
(to) **remove** [rɪ'mu:v] ausbauen, entfernen

reply *(n.)* [rɪ'plaɪ] Antwort
(to) **require** [rɪ'kwaɪə] benötigen
(to) **rescue** ['reskju:] befreien, retten
reunification [ˌri:ju:nɪfɪ'keɪʃn] Wiedervereinigung
(to) **revenge oneself** [rɪ'vendʒ] sich rächen
risk *(n.)* [rɪsk] Risiko
roar *(n.)* [rɔ:] Aufheulen
romantic [rəʊ'mæntɪk] romantisch
Romany, *pl.:* **Romanies** ['rɒməni, -z] Rom, Roma
rope [rəʊp] Seil
rotor arm ['rəʊtərɑ:m] Verteilerfinger
rubbish ['rʌbɪʃ] Müll
(to) **rumble** ['rʌmbl] rumpeln, donnern
(to) **run** [rʌn] betreiben
(to) **run out of petrol** kein Benzin mehr haben
run: on the run auf der Flucht
(to) **rush** [rʌʃ] rennen

S **safety** ['seɪfti] Sicherheit
scrapyard ['skræpjɑ:d] Schrottplatz
search [sɜ:tʃ] Suche, Nachforschungen
seat [si:t] Sitz
seat-belt ['si:tbelt] Sicherheitsgurt
secret *(n.)* ['si:krət] Geheimnis
secretly ['si:krətli] im Geheimen
semicircular [ˌsemi'sɜ:kjələ] halbkreisförmig
sensible ['sensəbl] vernünftig
sentence ['sentəns] Strafe
sergeant ['sɑ:dʒənt] Kriminalmeister/in
(to) **serve a prison sentence** [sɜ:v] eine Gefängnisstrafe verbüßen
service area ['sɜ:vɪs ˌeəriə] Tankstelle und Raststätte
service tunnel ['sɜ:vɪs ˌtʌnl] Versorgungstunnel
shadow ['ʃædəʊ] Schatten

share *(n.)* [ʃeə] Anteil
shocked [ʃɒkt] schockiert
(to) **shoplift** ['ʃɒplɪft] Ladendiebstahl begehen
shoplifter ['ʃɒplɪftə] Ladendieb/in
shoulder ['ʃəʊldə] Schulter
shout *(n.)* [ʃaʊt] Schrei
(to) **shut up** [ˌʃʌt‿'ʌp] den Mund halten
side: just to be on the safe side ['seɪf saɪd] um ganz sicher zu gehen
sight: in sight [saɪt] in Sicht
sightseeing tour ['saɪtsiːɪŋ tʊə] Stadtrundfahrt
silence: in silence ['saɪləns] schweigend
siren ['saɪrən] Sirene
skin [skɪn] Haut
slid: (to) **slide, slid, slid** [slaɪd, slɪd, slɪd] rutschen
(to) **slow down** [ˌsləʊ 'daʊn] langsamer fahren
small-time crook [ˌsmɔːltaɪm 'krʊk] kleine/r Gauner/in
(to) **smile** [smaɪl] lächeln
smile *(n.)* [smaɪl] Lächeln
smoking ['sməʊkɪŋ] Rauchen
(to) **sniff** [snɪf] schnuppern
sound *(n.)* [saʊnd] Geräusch
soundly: (to) **sleep soundly** ['saʊndli] tief schlafen
speeding ['spiːdɪŋ] Geschwindigkeitsüberschreitung
speedometer [spiː'dɒmɪtə] Tachometer
(to) **split up, split, split** [ˌsplɪt‿'ʌp, splɪt, splɪt] sich auflösen
(to) **spot** [spɒt] entdecken
spot: on the spot [spɒt] an Ort und Stelle
(to) **spy on sb.** [spaɪ] jm. nachspionieren
(to) **stare at each other** [steə] sich anstarren
starter motor ['stɑːtə ˌməʊtə] Anlasser
step [step] Stufe; Schritt
stiffly ['stɪfli] steif

(to) **stop dead** [ˌstɒp 'ded] abrupt stehen bleiben
string [strɪŋ] Schnur, Kette
(to) **stroke** [strəʊk] streicheln
(to) **struggle** ['strʌgl] sich abmühen
such [sʌtʃ] so, solch
Such as what? Was zum Beispiel?
supper ['sʌpə] Abendessen
supposing angenommen …
surely ['ʃʊəli, 'ʃɔːli] bestimmt
surprise: in surprise [sə'praɪz] überrascht
(to) **suspect sb.** [sə'spekt] jn. verdächtigen

T **tail-light** ['teɪllaɪt] Rücklicht
(to) **take notice of sb.** ['nəʊtɪs] jn. beachten
(to) **tease** [tiːz] aufziehen, hänseln
territory ['terətri] Revier, Gebiet
thank goodness [θæŋk 'gʊdnəs] Gott sei Dank
thief, *pl.:* **thieves** [θiːf, θiːvz] Dieb/in
torch [tɔːtʃ] Taschenlampe
trapeze [trə'piːz] Trapez
traveller ['trævələ] Landfahrer/in, Zigeuner/in
trial ['traɪəl] Prozess
(to) **be tricked** [trɪkt] hereingelegt werden
(to) **trust** [trʌst] vertrauen
(to) **turn off** [ˌtɜːn‿'ɒf] ausschalten
(to) **turn up** [ˌtɜːn‿'ʌp] auftauchen, kommen

U **unless** [ən'les] wenn … nicht
(to) **unlock** [ˌʌn'lɒk] aufschließen
unseen [ˌʌn'siːn] unsichtbar
use: (to) **be no use** [juːs] keinen Sinn haben
used: there used to be a phone box [juːst] früher gab es hier eine Telefonzelle

used-car dealer [ˌjuːzdˈkɑː ˌdiːlə] Gebrauchtwagen-händler/in
useless [ˈjuːsləs] unbrauchbar

V **van** [væn] Lieferwagen, Kastenwagen
vandal [ˈvændl] Rowdy
vehicle [ˈviːəkl] Fahrzeug
voice [vɔɪs] Stimme

W (to) **wail** [weɪl] heulen
(to) **walk off** [ˌwɔːk‿ˈɒf] weggehen
(to) **warn** [wɔːn] darauf aufmerksam machen
(to) **waste** [weɪst] vergeuden
while *(n.)* [waɪl] Weile
(to) **whine** [waɪn] jaulen, winseln
whistle *(n.)* [ˈwɪsl] Pfeife
(to) **whistle** [ˈwɪsl] pfeifen
wide [waɪd] weit
wing mirror [ˈwɪŋ ˌmɪrə] Außenspiegel
(to) **wish** [wɪʃ] wünschen
(to) **wonder** [ˈwʌndə] sich fragen
wooden [ˈwʊdn] Holz-
woodwork [ˈwʊdwɜːk] Werken mit Holz
workshop [ˈwɜːkʃɒp] Werkstatt

Y **yacht** [jɒt] Jacht
yachtsman, yachtsmen [ˈjɒtsmən, -mən] Segler
yard [jɑːd] Hof; *britisches Längenmaß* (= 0,91m)
yeah [jeə] ja
youth [juːθ] Jugend

Names

People's names

Darrow ['dærəʊ]
Gerry ['dʒeri]
Ilona [ɪ'ləʊnə]
Jake [dʒeɪk]
Jason ['dʒeɪsn]
Albert Johnson [ˌælbət 'dʒɒnsn]
Julia ['dʒu:liə]
Shorty Mulligan [ˌʃɔ:ti 'mʌlɪgən]
Sid/Sidney Mulligan [ˌsɪd/ˌsɪdni 'mʌlɪgən]
Patrick ['pætrɪk]
Mrs Pyne [paɪn]
Ray/Raymond George Smith [ˌreɪ/ˌreɪmənd ˌdʒɔ:dʒ 'smɪθ]
Rosso ['rɒsəʊ]
Shakespeare ['ʃeɪkspɪə]
Simmons ['sɪmənz]
Williams ['wɪljəmz]

Place names

Africa ['æfrɪkə]
Barbados [bɑ:'beɪdɒs]
Battersea ['bætəsi]
Belgium ['beldʒəm]
Bermondsey ['bɜ:mənzi]
Camberwell ['kæmbəwel]
Chelsea ['tʃelsi]
Clapham ['klæpəm]
Hampstead Heath [ˌhæmpstɪd 'hi:θ]
Heathrow [ˌhi:θ'rəʊ]

Jamaica [dʒə'meɪkə]
Kensington ['kenzɪŋtən]
Lavender Hill [ˌlævəndə 'hɪl]
Leicester ['lestə]
Marble Arch [ˌmɑːbl‿'ɑːtʃ]
Nine Elms [ˌnaɪn‿'elmz]
Newport Pagnell [ˌnjuːpɔːt 'pægnəl]
Oxfordshire ['ɒksfədʃə]
Pakistan [ˌpɑːkɪ'stɑːn]
St James's Park [sən ˌdʒeɪmzɪz 'pɑːk]
River Thames [ˌrɪvə 'temz]
Rotherhithe (Tunnel) [ˌrɒðəhaɪð 'tʌnl]
Trinidad ['trɪnɪdæd]
Wandsworth ['wɒnzwəθ]

Street names

Austin Rd. [ˌɒstɪn 'rəʊd]
Culvert Rd./Place [ˌkʌlvət 'rəʊd/'pleɪs]
Enid Street ['iːnɪd striːt]
Francis Chichester Way [ˌfrɑːnsɪs ˌtʃɪtʃɪstə 'weɪ]
Piccadilly [ˌpɪkə'dɪli]
Rowditch Lane [ˌrəʊdɪtʃ 'leɪn]
Versleigh Rd. [ˌvɜːsliː 'rəʊd]

Other names

Alpha Charlie [ˌælfə 'tʃɑːli]
Aston Martin [ˌæstən 'mɑːtɪn]
Eros Statue ['ɪərɒs ˌstætʃuː]
Evening Standard [ˌiːvnɪŋ 'stændəd]
Ford Escort [ˌfɔːd‿'eskɔːt]
Jaguar ['dʒægjuə]

Peter Pan [ˌpiːtə ˈpæn]
Riley [ˈraɪli]
Swatch [swɒtʃ]
Triumph Spitfire [ˌtraɪʌmf ˈspɪtfaɪə]
Woolworth's [ˈwʊlwəθs]
Yale key/lock [ˈjeɪl kiː/lɒk]